Gas-Securing Equipment

AF112388

Gas-Securing Equipment

Table of Contents

Chapter 1
Introduction   Page 4

Chapter 2
Oil and Gas Additives   Page 7

Chapter 3
Magnetic Devices   Page 10

Chapter 4
Air Injection Products   Page 12

Chapter 5
Be Wary of the Testimonials that a Product Offers   Page 15

Chapter 6
Gas Saving Devices and Products that can Work   Page 17

Chapter 7
Save Money on Gas with Hypermiling Strategies   Page 21

Chapter 8
Conclusion   Page 25

Chapter 1
Introduction

There are plenty of products on the market for consumers to chose from. Most of the time they evolve based on the needs of society. When there is a trend taking place then you will see many different products emerge that can meet the new need people have.

Some of them have been around for many years but people just don't notice them. They aren't recognized until there is a significant need for them. Older products may change how they advertise and even change the name of the product in order to get a facelift in the public eye.

It is no secret to anyone that gas prices have continued to rise to unbelievable prices over the past couple of years. While there has been a steady increase all along, nothing has taken place like it has in the past six months. It sees like the prices at the pumps are increasing every couple of days.

That has many consumers scared to death and scrambling for a solution. They aren't making more money but continue have more expenses to cover. The more your drive your vehicle they more you are affected by these increasing fuel prices. It can be a very scary time if you already have a thin budget to work with.

It may only be by a few cents but that quickly adds up to too much per gallon. The fact that the prices tend to go up every week isn't helping. In the end you are likely paying more money when you fill up than ever before. This has also lead to an increase in the cost of everything else.

That is because it is taking more money for suppliers to get it delivered. All of that price increase is being passed on to the consumer. Trucking companies have to pay more for fuel to get supplies to lumber yards, groceries and supplies to stores, and even to transport fuel to the gas stations. They can't stay in business if they don't increase what they charge for such deliveries.

As a result the places they are delivering materials to have to increase what they charge in order to make a profit. This is a continuous cycle with the final consumer getting the short end of the stick. This has resulted in people traveling less and buying fewer items that aren't essential.

With very little chance that gas prices are going to drop, people are looking for alternatives. That is why business entrepreneurs are offering a variety of gas saving devices. The controversy though is that some people believe they work while others are convinced they are nothing more than a scam.

There are hundreds of such products out there available and that is appealing to consumers. They are tired of paying high amounts for gas and they are willing to do all they can in order to find a way out of it. Advertisers of such products know this and they continue to appeal to the emotions of these consumers in order to sell more of their products.

Before you buy one of them you need to do your homework. You need to find out what other consumers have to say about it. You definitely don't want to waste your time or money on something that isn't going to be effective. There is no reason to hand over the cash until you know you are getting a legitimate product with a high level of credibility behind it.

The Federal Trade Commission has issued several warnings about the use of gas saving devices. Therefore it is very important for you to be sure you know what you are paying for. If it sounds too good to be true than more than likely it is. Don't find out after you have paid for the product.

The Federal Trade Commission has tested more than 100 products on the market that claim a person can save 20% or more on their gas expenses. However, this agency wasn't able to verify any of these products could offer those results or any significant benefit at all.

You may be familiar with particular fuel saving products that have been advertised. They all fall into particular categories depending on how you use them and what methods they incorporate. Keep reading to find out reliable information on each of these categories.

Chapter 2
Oil and Gas Additives

One of the most popular types of gas saving devices are oil and gas additives. Chances are you have seen many of them advertised in magazines and you can find them on the shelves of the stores you frequent. If you haven't noticed them before you should take a look for them.

One thing you will notice is that they all have claims that they can provide you with better gas mileage than you get right now. Some of them claim to be FDA approved and such but that isn't the case. It does make you wonder though why they are able to place such items on the shelves when the FDA denies approving such products.

Some of these are products you pour into your gas tank when you feel up at the pump. You simply put the contents into your tank first and then continue to fuel up as you normally would. Since it does take up some room it will reduce the amount of gas you have to put into it but not improve your overall miles per gallon that you will burn while operating your vehicle.

There are a variety of ingredients added to your gas when you pour such an additive into your gas tank. They include tin, magnesium, and platinum which these marketers will tell you is good for removing compounds that settle into the bottom of your gas tank.

Never use a fuel additive that contains acetone as it can damage plastic parts in your fuel system by dissolving them. Some individuals claim that a small amount of acetone won't harm your fuel system but it can be hard to gauge when you have gone over that amount. Also, it really hasn't been proven to help cut back on the cost of gas so that is quite a risk to be taking.

In general, these additive products won't harm your vehicle but generally aren't necessary to add. Such gas saving products are marketed in a way to give you the impression that you are getting something your gas tank needs to be more efficient.

That is the key selling point and many consumers take the bait. They go out and buy several bottles of this additive and keep it in their vehicle. Each time they approach the pump to fill up they dump a bottle of it in there thinking they are doing the right thing. However, doing so really isn't necessary.

This is because gasoline has ingredients in it that will naturally do the same thing without you adding anything. Even though these fuel additives are very reasonably priced they still seem to be a waste of money as they haven't been proven to be effective. The gas you have to pay for to move your vehicle is already taking care of the same concerns so why pay for something you don't need?

Those that are offered for the oil generally come already mixed in the oil for your car. You just add it like you would any other brand or type of oil. It is important that you always use the right grade of motor oil in order to get the most fuel mileage from your vehicle. You can find this information in your owners' manual as well as on the internet.

The understanding of gas savings behind these oils is that the lower velocity that is present the less friction will be created. However, you can really do severe damage to your vehicle if you are using something other than what it requires. You may end up needing to replace your entire engine before it is all said and done.

Some testing has shown changing the velocity of the oil doesn't seem to affect the operations of certain vehicles. As a consumer though you have to ask yourself if you are willing to take the chance that such a product may damage your vehicle. Most people will agree it isn't something they want to risk being on the losing side of.

There doesn't seem to be a good reason to take that risk either. There hasn't been any substantial evidence to suggest oil additives are going to increase your gas mileage. Yet these are very popular products that people continue to buy and place into their vehicle.

Oil and gas additives aren't very expensive and you can generally buy them at any location that sales automotive products. Most full stores offer oil, filters, and these various additives so you can get all the supplies you need for the maintenance of your vehicle at one time.

You may be tempted to buy such products that you see on the shelves while you are buying the other items you need. However, you need to be careful about what you put into your vehicle. It could end up doing more damage than good. You can read reviews about specific products out there online so it is a good idea to do so before you go ahead and purchase any of them.

Chapter 3
Magnetic Devices

Magnets are quite interesting because they have the ability to attract and repel due to the energy they create. We can all probably remember science experiments in school that dealt with magnets. They were actually very fun to play with and to see what they could do.

Magnets of all different sizes are used in our society for a variety of things. We use them to keep things on the refrigerator, to search for items, and to operate various types of devices. Many people view magnets as something scientific though so they assume it may be logical to try using them to save money when it comes to fuel costs.

Many consumers like this idea because they aren't adding anything to their vehicle in the form of a liquid which often makes them worried. The magnets can be added or removed any time you feel like it. They like the thought of being able to get results without the risk of ruining some part of their engine.

There is also the fact that you don't have to remember to buy them all the time. With additives you need to get a good supply of them and then remember to use them at the right times. With the magnets you can simply put them on once and then not worry about it again.

Magnets that are offered for reducing the amount of gas that your car uses will cost you between $15 and $40 so that isn't too much of an overall investment. They can improve your gas mileage ever so slightly but not enough that you will get any real savings out of it. We are talking 10th of a gallon when it comes to measuring the benefits.

These magnets are secured to the fuel line and are believed to change the molecular structure of the gasoline. As a result the types of metals that are used to ionize the fuel will no longer be there. This may all sound good in theory but the reality is that it doesn't do anything for your gas mileage that is significant enough for you to save any money.

Magnetic gas saving products often have the biggest claims when it comes to how much gas you can save. Many of them boost about a savings of 20% -25% but the testing on such products hasn't shown hardly any benefit at all, let alone something that substantial.

There is a popular TV show called MythBusters where they take certain products and test them out to see what the results are. They did a show about the use of magnets to increase fuel mileage a while back. You can see parts of it on their website if you missed it.

Several different brands of magnets advertised for saving gas were tried out but the results were similar with all of the ones they tried. They were able to control the variables and tried the use of the magnets under a variety of different conditions.

They didn't find them to be difficult to put on the vehicle or to remove. They also didn't find them to offer any significant benefit in the area of gas mileage from them. So the best bet is to skip these types of gas saving devices and use your money for something else.

Chapter 4
Air Injection Products

Many of the gas saving devices on the market right now fall into the category of a vortex generator. The name of it sounds like something very fancy and that would be complicated to work with. Once you understand the concept of it though it is easy to see how people would assume it could help cut down their use of gas.

This allows there to be air mixed between the air cleaner and the intake manifold. The process resembles a tornado but on a much smaller scale. There isn't anything type of additive with various ingredients being added to your vehicle which makes consumers happy.

Since there is an unlimited supply of air nothing has to be added to it later on either. These products claim to work by mixing more air with the gas in your vehicle than what is normally found in it. This is to allow it to burn cleaner when it enters the combustion chamber.

Yet what you will find is that your speed is reduced due to this method and so that can result in gas being saved. For those that drive over 60 miles per hour the most savings will be evident.

However, if you plan to be taking that vehicle on a highway with a speed limit of 75 miles per hour you will have a hard time getting to that speed as well as maintaining it. Your vehicle may start to run sluggish which can mean something with it isn't being properly operated like it should.

Your vehicle will have to work very hard and that can result in more wear on it. If you have to slow down or stop often it will also reduce fuel efficiency. When you consider the distance a person may travel for fun or to get back and forth to work at those higher speeds it can really be a recipe for disaster for our vehicle. Some of the air injection products offered claim that they can create more heat, and that reduces friction.

As a result of less friction there is less fuel consumed. It is said that there is less work for the liquid gas to be changed into a vapor. The understanding of this particular technique is complex to many people. Therefore they don't look into it any further.

What is often ironic about gas saving devices and products is that is seems the more complicated they are to understand the more people invest in them. The general consensus of this is that it must be some scientific formula that will work and so it doesn't matter if the consumer understands it or not.

Well, you can be sure that the manufacturers and the marketers know this. If the gas saving device is too simple then it won't hold water with most people. Add some tricky terms though and a process that is complex to follow and it will seem logical in many ways. After all not everyone knows ways to save money on gas so they may be on to something.

Regardless of if you understand what that process entails or not, the testing that has been done on many products by professional organizations shows they don't really work. There isn't enough significance with that process to allow you to save money on your gas expenses.

You need to get the name of the particular product you are interested in and do your own research on it as well. Chances are there have been reviews of it from individual consumers. You will also find those done by experts that aren't biased one way or the other. They call it as they see it simply by monitoring their gas mileage before and after using it on a particular vehicle.

All of the data that they use is recorded and shared so there isn't any secret about how they derived at their final report on things. It is hard to argue with such testing methods when you can see they have done every single step by the book and not gotten the promised results with the given product.

One of these testing gurus is Popular Mechanics. They are well known for offering information and advice about various types of vehicles. They stay on top of current issues and events including high gas prices. They aren't about to allow their loyal readers to be taken for a ride to listen to what they have to say.

There are many air injection products for gas saving offered on the market. Yet according to Popular Mechanics many of them never even get around to actually adding more air to the fuel like they claim. They believe it just isn't possible for this to really take place with the design of the vehicles system.

This is due to the fact that there is likely to be too much space between where they air intake is and where the fuel is mixed. It doesn't really matter which type of vehicle you are driving around in, this set up is standard. You can have it modified which will cost you a great deal of money which we will cover in chapter 6.

Chapter 5
Be Wary of the Testimonials that a Product Offers

Testimonials are a sure fire way to motivate people to buy what you have for sale with any type of product. You will find that many gas saving devices feature such testimonials from very satisfied consumers. Before you let this make the decision to buy them for you there are a few things you need to know.

While these testimonials may be real, they often don't show the entire story. For example someone may start their testimonial letter out by saying they got an addition 5 miles per gallon from their car as soon as they started using the product. That is a legitimate claim they have made. Yet the company doesn't include all of the information that was provided, jus the part that really gets the attention of the reader.

That letter may have gone on to say how they have gotten their car repaired and tuned up. It can also contain information on how they are driving differently. Those additional factors are likely a big part of what is allowing them to get an addition 5 miles per gallon.

So it isn't just that they started using a particular gas saving device and it make that huge impact for them. There is no way for a consumer to know the rest of the story from what is written. There is nothing you can do about this marketing method either.

Since they aren't lying about what the consumer said they can't be fined or face any repercussions. There is no law that says they have to print the entire testimonial. They just have to be from real people and be in the same words as what was originally written by the person. So

So they can begin with the beginning, middle, or end of a particular testimonial. They take the pieces they want and leave the rest of it. Therefore I caution you to put too much credibility behind the testimonials that are offered for such products.

There may be some truth to them but remember that they only publish what they want you to see in regards to their product. All those letters they get that are complaints never will be part of their advertising either. Those people may get a refund or nothing at all.

You may be able to find the discontent though with various gas saving products by reading information online. People are very willing to share their experiences in such areas with others so that they won't fall into the same trap. This can save you money so pay attention to the information that can be accessed with any search engine.

You also need to understand that what may work well for one vehicle isn't right for another. It is the same concept that applies to products such as medications and even diet pills. There are plenty of people who claim to get results but for the majority of the population they aren't effective enough to make a difference.

This is due to the fact that each vehicle has significant variables. Even the same exact make, model, and year of a vehicle may have different gas mileage associated with it. The way in which the car is cared for and the driving habits of those who use it also have to be taken into consideration.

Chapter 6
Gas Saving Devices and Products that can Work

So far the outlook for gas saving devices and products has been quite grim. The major vehicle manufacturers continue to try to develop something that can work in order to make their cars more appealing to consumers. Built in fuel savings can be accomplished not with gadgets but with attention given in the areas of the design of the vehicle as well as the engine.

This is because it is much easier to sale a vehicle when it has many features that consumers will be looking for. A great style of car on the outside, nice paint job, and stylish interior simply isn't enough anymore. It is important to note though that these big corporations with highly educated engineers haven't found the secret to significant gas savings methods.

If they were out there then they would be incorporating the design on these newer models of vehicles. That reality alone should really get consumers to wake up and see what has been taking place around them all this time. They need to stop paying for ineffective products that are being sold due to the need people have to really save some money on gas.

Sure there are some ideas that have worked out well to accomplish significant gas savings. There isn't any reason to fully discount everything across the board. The biggest issue though are that you can't implement them without spending far more money than you will ever save. The ends don't justify the means and so consumers are stuck right back where they started.

Here are some examples of ways you can save money on fuel costs but that are just too expensive to move forward with. There have been successful attempts to modify the calibration of the engine in some models of vehicles to save on fuel. However, this process has to be done by a certified mechanic.

The price tag is between $10,000 and $12,000 which is often more than the value of the vehicle for many individuals. You would need to keep that car for at least 12 years and be putting at least 1,500 miles on the vehicle per month during that span of time to get your investment back.

The amount of fuel savings isn't substantial enough to justify that type of investment in the vehicle. You won't be able to get a return on it because you won't save that much money in fuel over the course of the time you own that vehicle. Very few people keep a regularly used vehicle for that length of time. There is also the issue that if it is involved in an accident and can't be driven you are definitely out all the money you invested in this process.

It does have some value in our society though for those with a great deal of money to spend in order to use as little gas as possible. The process has been done to many professional vehicles though including semi trucks and race cars. When you consider a semi truck generally gets about 4-7 miles per gallon you really need to maximize the fuel efficiency.

In racing events every little bit of fuel you can reserve will give you an edge over the competition. For example the NASCAR drivers need to be able to evaluate when they will go in for fuel. Being able to go an extra lap over the competition can make the difference between coming in 5th and coming in 1st.

Most consumers are interested in the gas saving devices for their own personal vehicles though not those used commercially or for sporting events such as racing. There are a couple of devices you can have installed inside of your vehicle that do show a very small improvement. There are accessory driver modifiers which will periodically turn off devices including the air conditioning at certain times.

These can be effective if you have many accessories that will result in higher fuel costs. There are also censors that will notify you of behaviors you engage in that can increase your fuel consumption. For example if you need to shift to a lower gear or you need to reduce your speed.

This can be helpful if you want to make changes to your driving behaviors but you often need a reminder to assist you with it. You won't be as likely to continue slipping into those older modes of behavior because you will have a constant way to remember it while behind the wheel of the vehicle.

Again, both of these types of devices are extremely expensive to install. They can range from $7,000 to $15,000. There doesn't seem to be enough of a fuel savings to warrant installing them for most people.

Perhaps there will be future car models that offer them built in when you buy them. Even so, those models of cars are going to be more expensive than what is offered without them. The manufacturer of these vehicles is going to have to pass that cost on to the person who buys it.

What holds manufacturers back from doing so is that they need to have very competitive prices. There are too many different makes and models of vehicles that people can purchase. When price is a factor consumers aren't going to pay for higher priced vehicles and so they have to balance what is practical and profitable for them into that overall equation.

Based on this information, there doesn't seem to be and affordable gas saving devices out there that would really improve your gas mileage and cut back on your expenses in this area. It appears that if you want to make such changes you are going to have to take matters into your own hands.

Researchers may be on the right track though so one day it is possible that they will come up with something both effective and affordable for the average person to purchase. Of course that doesn't leave us with a very pretty picture right now does it?

Don't despair though as there are some things you can start doing right away to improve your gas mileage. They aren't gimmicks or crazy ideas that someone else is going to make money off of. They are realistic approaches that you can certainly see benefits from in a short span of time.

Chapter 7
Save Money on Gas with Hypermiling Strategies

With all of the negativity out there about gas saving devices and products that just don't work, you may be better off to put your time and money into other efforts that have been known to work rather well.

You can be sure if a really effective gas saving device does come onto the market it will be in the news, online, and people will be talking about it. In the mean time do what you can to save yourself as much money as you can. It can prevent you from being as stressed out when you see that gas gauge towards empty.

A very effective method you may want to incorporate into your gas saving efforts is hypermiling. It means you will be able to change some of your behaviors, get your vehicle in top operating shape, and maximize fuel efficiency. You will also be able to monitor your progress without any gadgets.

This is a proven way for you to save money without buying any type of product at all. In addition, it will help you to have a vehicle that last longer. You won't be needing a new one any time soon when it is well maintained. It will also help to reduce the risk of vehicle related accidents.

How often do you change the oil on your vehicle? This should be a standard practice every 3,000 miles or every 3 months. Which every one you get to first is what you go with. Most places that change your oil will put a sticker on the inside of the windshield. It will tell you the date and the mileage so you can easily view that information.

Having the right amount of air in your tires will help to reduce the amount of fuel you use as well. You need to check your owner's manual to see how much pounds of pressure you should have in each of them. Too much or too little isn't safe either so always keep a close eye on this.

Get your vehicle a tune up every six months to a year as well depending on how many miles you put on it. At this time they can do a complete inspection for you. Don't wait until something is really wrong with your vehicle before you get it looked at.

A leaking fuel injector, clogged air filter, or an old oxygen sensor won't prevent your vehicle from operating. However, it will increase the amount of fuel you have to use in order to get around. It is more cost effective to repair or replace these items in order to save you money in the long run.

By maintaining a constant speed you will use less fuel in you vehicle. It is when you accelerate and slow down all the time that you end up using more of it. If that is your style of driving then you can modify it. Stop speeding to get places on time and plan better so you can leave earlier.

Instead of rushing to pass the cars in front of you set your cruise control. This way you can stay at a constant speed. You also want to leave enough room between you and the car in front of you. This will require less breaking and so your car won't use as much fuel to get back into motion again.

Making changes to your regular routine is also a big part of hypermiling. Think about carpooling to work and for your children's activities whenever possible. This will reduce the amount of trips you make per week in your vehicle.

You also need to schedule errands and other outings so you aren't covering the same ground over and over again. Plan when you will go to the grocery store and everything you need for a one or two week period. This way you won't be having to go back and forth for select ingredients to complete your meals.

Hypermiling has become quite popular as a method for saving money on gas. It doesn't require buying any type of device and most of the options are extremely affordable or cost nothing at all. An oil change generally runs about $30 which is no big deal. Other vehicle repairs are going to cost more but you still need to get them taken care of.

It is great if you can do the work on your own as you will only have to pay for the cost of the parts. When a mechanic does it for you there is also the cost of labor included. The sooner you get such repairs done though the faster you can start saving money on your gas expenses. It will also help you get more life out of your vehicle.

These strategies are definitely worth looking into to see how you can benefit from them. Since they are supported by the United States government, the Environmental Protection Agency, and the Department of Public Safety that makes them very credible too in the eyes of the consumer.

Hypermiling has proven to be much more valuable for those interested in saving money on gas than various types of devices and products on the market. If you want to see how they can work for you get a tank of gas. Keep track of the mileage and how many gallons of fuel you put in.

When you are out of gas determine how many miles you went on that tank of gas. When you divide that amount by the number of gallons you purchased you get the amount of miles per gallon.

Now Implement one or two of the hypermiling strategies before you fill up the second time. Keep track of your miles per gallon using that same formula. You will see some differences and hopefully that will encourage you to continue with these methods. You can also consider implementing a couple more of them to give yourself even better gas mileage.

Chapter 8
Conclusion

With gas prices continuing to soar, consumers are looking for every possible way to save money on it. If you take a look at what is offered you will find plenty of different gas saving devices offered. Most of them don't seem to be very effective though. This is quite disheartening when you consider that this is a $25 million industry in 2007 alone.

According to the experts, about 95% of the gas saving products offered don't stand up to the claims they make. They also don't make enough of a difference to justify buying them. That can be extremely disappointing but that is the reality of it. So why do so many consumers continue to buy them?

First, they want to believe they work because they do want to be able to save money on their fuel costs. That is certainly understandable as we have all been affected by the high prices. They also see so many of the products on the market that they assume they must be working or they wouldn't be offered. This is why such products continue to sell at very high rates.

Those are the consumers who aren't taking the time to do their research before they invest in them either. They many end up purchasing several different gas saving products and devices before they finally see the big picture and how ineffective they have been.

They read the testimonials with the products or see the advertisements and decide that is what they need to purchase. They are in a hurry to access it and to benefit from it. Instead they end up losing their money and being disappointed. You should always pursue a refund when such gas saving products fail to give you the results that they advertise.

Some of the research conducted by Popular Mechanics has even proven that a handful of these so called gas saving devices actually end up increasing the amount of fuel that you use. That certainly isn't the type of result you want to get from something like this that you pay for to use in your vehicles.

Therefore consumers really need to take their time choosing such products that are right for them. Take the time to read information online and see what is really going on with them. The information you get from other consumers is going to prove to be extremely valuable to you.

It should carry more weight with you than the business advertisements for such products. These will be honest reviews from real people who have been in your position before. It is quite likely the information they offer will prevent you from making a purchase of that particular gas saving device.

Making a well informed decision before you invest in this type of product is very wise. You don't want to become frustrated or disappointed due to the results you get. It is also a good idea to look for those that offer a money back guarantee. This way you will be able to get your investment back if you aren't 100% satisfied with what you purchase.

There is no argument that everyone needs to do what they can in order to save money on gas right now. But that doesn't necessarily mean buying gas saving products is the way to go. Many consumers have been able to successfully incorporate the concepts of hypermiling to save money without any real investment.

For example, simply changing your driving habits can result in a significant amount of gas being conserved. In the end you will have to decide which gas saving methods are right for you. There are certainly many different choices that you are being offered right now.

From what has been reported from reputable agencies, there aren't really effective gas saving devices and gadgets out there to really help you. There are plenty of in depth reports online about specific products you can read. This is better than buying them and trying them out on your own.

It can be frustrating paying high gas prices but be careful what you get encouraged to buy on the market during this difficult time. Your best bet is going to be to keep your car running properly and improving your driving habits.

www.ingramcontent.com/pod-product-compliance
Lightning Source LLC
LaVergne TN
LVHW020508080526
838202LV00057B/6235